RED-HOT
SELLING

RED-HOT
SELLING

Power Techniques That Win
Even the Toughest Sale

Paul S. Goldner

AMACOM

American Management Association

New York • Atlanta • Brussels • Chicago • Mexico City • San Francisco
Shanghai • Tokyo • Toronto • Washington, D. C.

Bulk discounts available. For details visit:
www.amacombooks.org/go/specialsales
Or contact special sales:
Phone: 800-250-5308
Email: specials@amanet.org
View all the AMACOM titles at: www.amacombooks.org

This publication is designed to provide accurate and authoritative information in regard to the subject matter covered. It is sold with the understanding that the publisher is not engaged in rendering legal, accounting, or other professional service. If legal advice or other expert assistance is required, the services of a competent professional person should be sought.

Library of Congress Cataloging-in-Publication Data

Goldner, Paul S.
    Red-hot selling : power techniques that win even the toughest sale / Paul S. Goldner.
      p. cm.
    Includes bibliographical references and index.
    ISBN-13: 978-0-8144-7353-5
    ISBN-10: 0-8144-7353-9
    1. Selling.   2. Sales presentations.   I. Title.
    HF5438.25G6423   2010
    658.85—dc22

                                                    2009029260

About AMA
American Management Association (www.amanet.org) is a world leader in talent development, advancing the skills of individuals to drive business success. Our mission is to support the goals of individuals and organizations through a complete range of products and services, including classroom and virtual seminars, webcasts, webinars, podcasts, conferences, corporate and government solutions, business books and research. AMA's approach to improving performance combines experiential learning—learning through doing—with opportunities for ongoing professional growth at every step of one's career journey.

Printing number

10 9 8 7 6 5 4 3 2 1